TERRORISM IN TODAY'S WORLD

September 11
and Radical Islamic Terrorism

PAUL BREWER

CURRICULUM CONSULTANT: MICHAEL M. YELL
National Board Certified Social Studies Teacher,
Hudson Middle School, Hudson, Wisconsin

WORLD ALMANAC® LIBRARY

Please visit our web site at: www.worldalmanaclibrary.com
For a free color catalog describing World Almanac® Library's list of high-quality books
and multimedia programs, call 1-800-848-2928 (USA) or 1-800-387-3178 (Canada).
World Almanac® Library's fax: (414) 332-3567.

Library of Congress Cataloging-in-Publication Data

Brewer, Paul.
   September 11 and radical Islamic terrorism / Paul Brewer.
     p. cm. – (Terrorism in today's world)
   Includes bibliographical references and index.
   ISBN 0-8368-6560-X (lib. bdg.)
   ISBN 0-8368-6567-7 (softcover)
   1. September 11 Terrorist Attacks, 2001–Juvenile literature.
   2. Islamic fundamentalism–Juvenile literature. I. Title: September eleven and
radical Islamic terrorism. II. Title. III. Series
   HV6432.7.B745   2006
   973.931–dc22   2005043692

This North American edition first published in 2006 by
World Almanac® Library
A Member of the WRC Media Family of Companies
330 West Olive Street, Suite 100
Milwaukee, WI 53212 USA

Managing Editor: Tim Cooke
Designer: Steve Wilson
Picture Researcher: Laila Torsun
World Almanac® Library editor: Alan Wachtel
World Almanac® Library art direction: Tammy West
World Almanac® Library design: Dave Kowalski
World Almanac® Library production: Jessica Morris and Robert Kraus

Picture credits: Front cover: Corbis: Reuters. BRG: 6; Corbis: Bettmann 27, Christophe Calais
/ In Visu 40, Kevin Fleming 24, National Security News Service/Handout /Reuters 29, Reuters 4/5
12/13, 20/21, 42, Shaul Schwarz 36; FEMA: Jocelyn Augustino 8; Getty Images: Robert Nickelsbug
15; Rex Features: KMLA 19, MAI 35, Marbella Photo 31, Sipa Press 10, 17, 38; Topham
Picturepoint: 25, 32/33.

Printed in the United States of America

1 2 3 4 5 6 7 8 9 10 09 08 07 06

CONTENTS

Cover photo: United Airlines Flight 175 crashes into the South Tower of the World Trade Center on September 11, 2001; the North Tower already burns after an earlier attack.

CHAPTER ONE

September 11, 2001

The aim of terrorism is to spread terror. Terrorists seek to achieve their aims by using violence to make large numbers of people afraid. Terrorist groups are usually small, and their acts, such as bombings and kidnappings, do not usually cause as much death and destruction as do acts of violence in war. Their acts, however, are planned to make large groups of people afraid enough to give in to their demands. Terrorists' aims vary: some want to create an independent state, for example, while others believe that they are acting from religious motives. Sometimes, as with the attackers of September 11, 2001 (or what became known in the media as "9/11"), religious zeal is combined with hatred of the economic and cultural influence of the West. The 9/11 attackers were Islamists, Muslims who believe that all aspects of society should be based on Islamic laws, including politics and daily life. They also hate the United States, because of its alliance with Israel and its military presence in the Middle East and elsewhere.

American Airlines Flight 11

At 7:59 A.M. on Tuesday, September 11, 2001, American Airlines Flight 11 took off from Boston's Logan International Airport for Los Angeles. About forty-five minutes later the Boeing 767 crashed into the North Tower of the World Trade Center in New York City. What at first seemed like a tragic accident turned out to be the first part of the single worst act of terrorism ever carried out on U.S. soil.

The last radio communication with the crew of Flight 11 came fifteen minutes into the flight. Soon

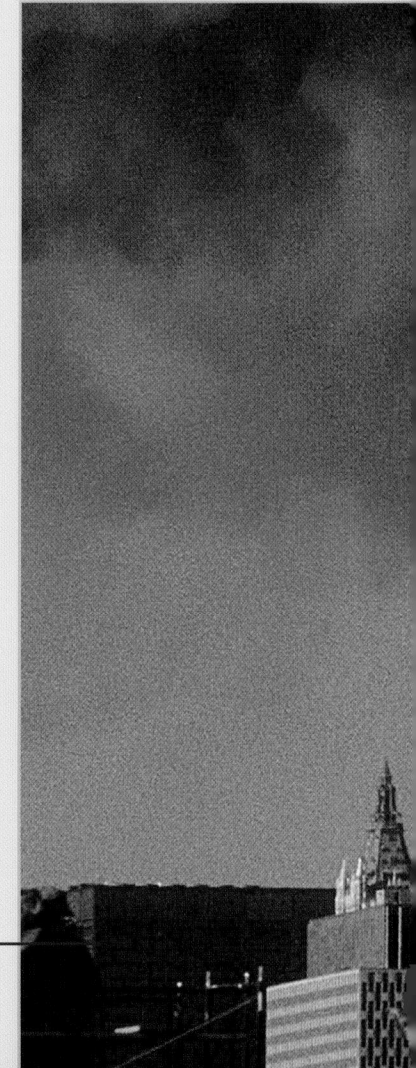

▼ A fireball erupts as United Airlines Flight 175 hits the South Tower at 9:03 A.M. Smoke already billows from the North Tower.

afterward, two flight attendants used cell phones to call airline staff in Boston to say that the airplane had been hijacked. A group of five Middle Eastern attackers had killed a passenger and stabbed two flight attendants. While the attendants gave details of the hijackers' seat numbers to help people on the ground identify them, some of the hijackers broke into the cockpit of the plane. The others used pepper spray or Mace in the front cabin to force the passengers and flight attendants to the back of the aircraft.

At 8:25 A.M., the hijackers in the cockpit tried to tell the passengers to stay in their seats. Instead of using the aircraft intercom, however, they mistakenly broadcast the message to air traffic controllers in Boston. The aircraft was now being flown by a hijacker. By 8:44 A.M., the airliner was flying toward New York City and descending fast. One of the flight attendants on the phone to the ground said, "I see water and buildings. . . ." A little later she added, "We are flying very, very low. We are flying way too low." At 8:46:40, American Airlines Flight 11 flew into the North Tower of the World Trade Center, one of the tallest buildings in the world, killing all ninety-two people

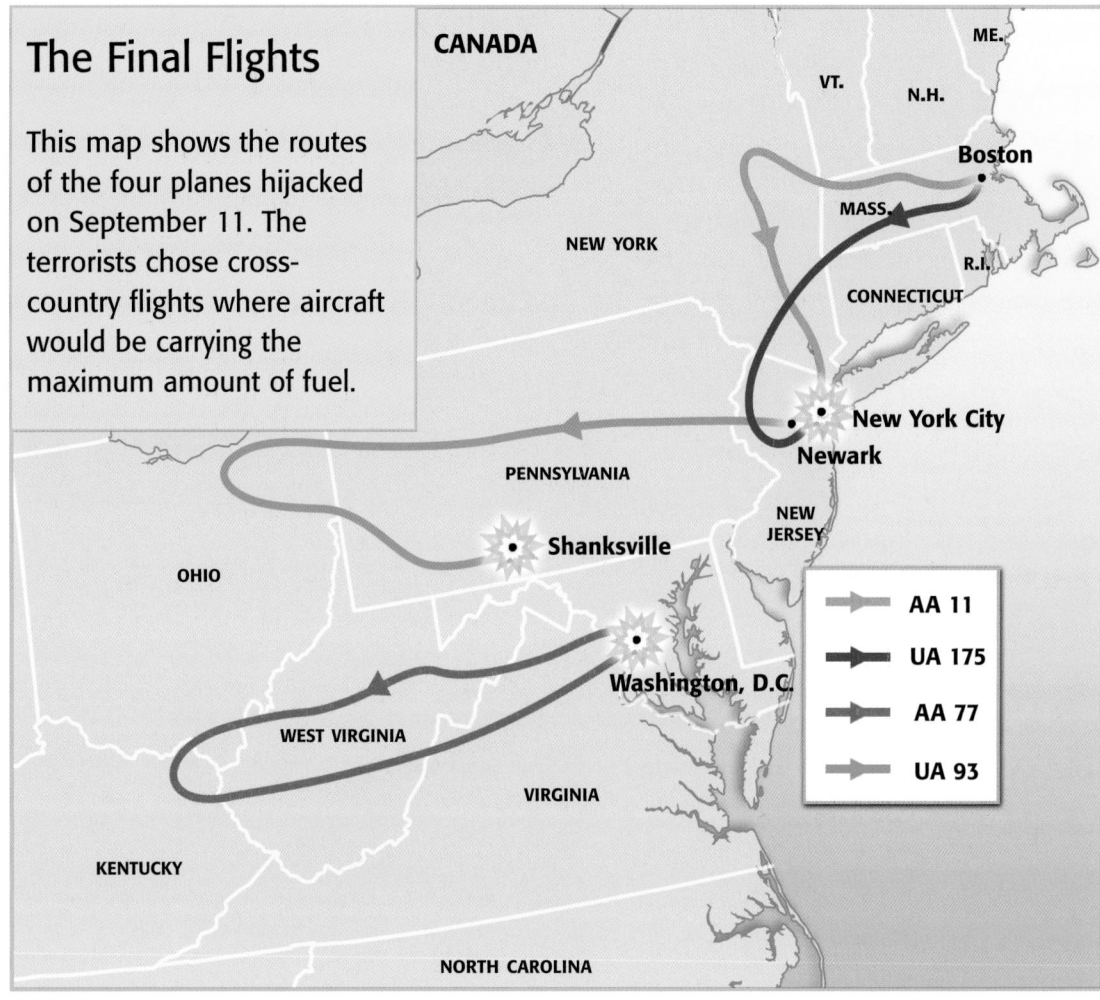

The Final Flights

This map shows the routes of the four planes hijacked on September 11. The terrorists chose cross-country flights where aircraft would be carrying the maximum amount of fuel.

CANADA

ME.

VT.

N.H.

Boston

MASS.

NEW YORK

R.I.

CONNECTICUT

New York City

Newark

PENNSYLVANIA

NEW JERSEY

OHIO

Shanksville

WEST VIRGINIA

Washington, D.C.

VIRGINIA

KENTUCKY

NORTH CAROLINA

AA 11

UA 175

AA 77

UA 93

on board and an unknown number in the building.

United Airlines Flight 175

The crash into the North Tower of the World Trade Center was only the start of the attack. Two more airplanes with hijackers aboard were already in the air. United Airlines Flight 175 had left Boston's Logan International Airport at 8:14 A.M.; it was another Boeing 767, bound for Los Angeles. Again flight attendants and passengers used cell phones to report events to the ground.

The hijackers took over the aircraft and gained entry to the cockpit, where they turned the plane toward New York City. One passenger called his father and said that he believed the hijackers planned to fly the airplane into a building. At 9:03 A.M., the United Airlines plane struck the South Tower of the World Trade Center in a huge fireball. All sixty-five people on board were killed, as well as an unknown number in the building.

Meanwhile, at 8:46 A.M., in response to the report of the hijacking of Flight

11, two F-15 fighter planes had taken off from Otis Air Force Base in Massachusetts. They were instructed to shoot down the hijacked airplane if it seemed as if it would fly into a target on the ground. They were too late. The order was issued at about the same time Flight 11 struck the North Tower. By the time the fighters got near New York City, Flight 175 had already struck the South Tower. More fighter planes were scrambled from Langley Air Force Base near Washington, D.C., but they did not have time to play any part in the unfolding drama in the skies. The U.S. air defense network had not had enough warning to be able to keep the hijackers from making their attacks.

Target: Pentagon

While smoke billowed from the towers of the World Trade Center, another airplane was heading for a different target. Five hijackers had boarded Los Angeles-bound American Airlines Flight 77 at Dulles International Airport near Washington, D.C., which took off at 8:20 A.M. About half an hour later, over Ohio, the hijackers seized the airplane and turned it back toward the capital. Again, people on board used cell phones to describe the events to people on the ground.

Reactions Around the World

Allies of the United States rallied to support the country after the attacks. Canada's prime minister, Jean Chrétien, said, "It is impossible to fully comprehend the evil that would have conjured up such a cowardly and depraved assault." With U.S. air space closed, Chrétien opened his country as a landing site for the many flights bound for the United States.

Pope John Paul II described the attacks as "a dark day for humanity, a terrible affront to human dignity." The leaders of Britain, Germany, and Russia expressed sympathy for the United States and condemned the hijackers. The French newspaper Le Monde declared, "We are all American today."

Outside of Europe, expressions of sympathy came to the United States from leaders of Mexico, Colombia, China, Japan, and many other countries. Many people throughout the Islamic world also condemned the attacks. Palestinian leader Yasser Arafat, who was an outspoken critic of U.S. support for the state of Israel, made a high-profile expression of sympathy. At the same time, however, some Palestinians in the West Bank town of Nablus were filmed celebrating the attacks on the United States in the streets.

Ordinary people around the world also expressed their sympathy. Huge numbers took to the streets of Bangladesh, Germany, Canada, Japan, and India to mourn the deaths.

Dulles Airport detected the aircraft flying at high speed and low altitude at 9:32 A.M. Five minutes later it, crashed into the Pentagon, the headquarters of the U.S. Department of Defense. The impact killed everyone on board and more than one hundred civilian and military personnel in the building.

The Crash of Flight 93

On the ground, panic and confusion reigned. When the second aircraft flew into the South Tower of the World Trade Center, it became clear that the first crash had not been an accident. The attack on the Pentagon was more evidence that a coordinated operation was under way, but no one knew how

many more hijacked aircraft might be in the air.

News of the attacks reached the flight crew of United Airlines Flight 93 about forty-five minutes into their journey from Newark, New Jersey, to San Francisco. A couple of minutes later, at 9:28 A.M., hijackers took over the aircraft. Passengers who used cell phones to call their relatives learned about the attack on the World Trade Center. Realizing that their plane was also likely to be used to attack a target on the ground, they tried to save their own lives and possibly many others.

The passengers fought the hijackers to try to recapture the aircraft. The terrorist flying the plane rolled it around violently to stop them. When they managed to force the cockpit door open, the pilot either deliberately or accidentally crashed the aircraft. It came down at 10:02 A.M. in a field near Shanksville, Pennsylvania, killing

▼ Rescue workers examine the site where American Airlines Flight 77 struck the Pentagon in Washington, D.C. The attack killed a total of 184 people on the plane and on the ground.

everyone on board. A later investigation concluded that the target of Flight 93 was either the White House or the Capitol in Washington, D. C. Only the brave action of the passengers and crew prevented the attack.

Brave Rescuers

As soon as the World Trade Center and the Pentagon had been struck, police and firefighters in New York and Washington, D.C., rushed to the disaster sites. Because the Pentagon building is only four stories high, emergency workers there were able to establish quickly the extent of the damaged area and begin evacuating casualties and survivors.

In New York City the rescuers faced a far more difficult task. The World Trade Center's twin towers each had 110 floors; they were each over 1,000 feet (300 m) tall. The airplanes had struck high up in the buildings: between the ninety-third and ninety-ninth floors of the North Tower and between the seventy-seventh and eighty-fifth floors of the South Tower. Fireballs raced through elevator shafts and stairwells. Vast amounts of fuel spilled from the airplanes and ignited. Clouds of smoke billowed outside and inside the buildings. Above the floors where the planes struck, stairs were blocked and escape was impossible. In the heat and smoke, some people preferred to jump to their deaths to avoid being burned alive.

When the first firefighters arrived at the scene, they did not know what the conditions were like high above them or whether emergency equipment, such as automatic fire extinguishers, was working. Because elevators in both towers were disabled, many firefighters had to use the stairs to climb up toward the impact sites. The New York Fire Department and Police Department set up command posts at

International Victims

The majority of the victims on September 11, 2001, were Americans, but more than two hundred of the dead came from other countries. The fifty thousand people who worked in the World Trade Center every day included many who worked for foreign companies. This list shows the number of victims from each country other than the United States:

Country	Number	Country	Number
Australia	1	Italy	4
Belgium	1	Ivory Coast	1
Brazil	3	Jamaica	16
Britain	67	Japan	23
China	2	Lebanon	3
Colombia	17	Mexico	14
Congo	2	Moldova	1
Ecuador	3	Nigeria	1
France	1	Peru	5
Germany	5	Philippines	15
Ghana	2	Portugal	3
Guyana	3	Russia	1
Haiti	2	Sweden	1
Honduras	1	Taiwan	1
India	12	Ukraine	1
Indonesia	1	Uzbekistan	1
Ireland	1	Venezuela	1
Israel	2		

Why the Towers Fell

The towers of the World Trade Center were built to withstand almost any kind of disaster. The hijackers, however, chose aircraft that were beginning long flights, so they were carrying the maximum amount of fuel. When the planes hit the towers, the fuel created fireballs that generated such high temperatures that the steel girders supporting the towers began to soften and melt.

The fires burned at different speeds in the two towers. After nearly an hour in the South Tower and an hour and three-quarters in the North Tower, the softened girders buckled and gave way. As the floors above the fires collapsed and pancaked, the floors below were unable to bear the weight and collapsed in turn. In the South Tower, where the impact was lower, some middle floors gave way first and the top of the building tipped slightly sideways before it collapsed downward. The whole process was very fast, taking only ten seconds for each tower.

floor after the plane struck described what happened when she got to the ground level: "All of a sudden the power shut off and the lights went out. The police yelled 'Run!' Then something behind me collapsed. The building was starting to come down. All you saw was black, it was so dark. Now everybody was screaming. I got out with a coworker. I grabbed his hand and we headed out together."

Police, firefighters, and many workers in the North Tower were unaware what had happened. They were

the foot of the towers and began to evacuate thousands of people from the floors below where the planes had hit.

At 9:58 A.M., the South Tower collapsed with a roar and a huge cloud of dust, killing everyone still inside and more people outside. A worker who had taken over forty minutes to walk down from her office on the eightieth

▶ People flee from the World Trade Center as the South Tower collapses in a huge cloud of dust. The choking dust spread to cover much of Lower Manhattan.

ordered to get out of the building, but radio problems prevented the order from reaching everyone. At 10:28 A.M., the North Tower collapsed.

Survivors and onlookers fled as thick clouds of dust filled the streets. An eyewitness in a nearby street recalled, "A cloud of black ash overcame us. You could not see your hands."

Nearly 3,000 people—passengers, aircrew, office workers, and rescuers—died in the terrorist attacks on September 11, 2001. At the World Trade Center, the total number of dead was 2,792, with an additional 2,261 injured. At the Pentagon, 184 died and 76 more were wounded. Flight 93 had 44 people on board, all of whom died when the plane crashed. As New Yorkers cared for the wounded and searched for the dead among the ruins of the World Trade Center, the nation wondered who had carried out the attacks.

A Nation Responds

The American people went into a state of collective shock on September 11, 2001. People outside of the attacked cities watched the news in horror. Baseball games and other events were canceled. U.S. air space was closed and all flights were grounded, trapping people who were traveling on business or vacation away from home. The Capitol was evacuated, and government offices in Washington, D.C., were closed. Parents and teachers across the country tried comforting their children, many of whom had watched the attacks unfold on television and been deeply disturbed by what they had seen. Schools offered counseling and support to help students deal with the trauma.

New York State Education Commissioner Richard Mills visited a school that had a large number of Muslim students. They were also in shock but, in addition, soon faced harassment when it became known that the terrorists had been Muslims. Meanwhile, prayer services and vigils were held throughout the country.

The mayor of New York City, Rudolph Giuliani, rallied New Yorkers to begin the task of recovery. Many people offered their support to the emergency workers, by taking food to firehouses, for example. Emergency workers were cheered as they drove through the streets to Ground Zero, as the site of the World Trade Center became known. The phrase refers to the spot at the center of a nuclear explosion.

One of the most visible responses to the tragedy was the appearance in Lower Manhattan of countless leaflets with pictures and descriptions of people missing after the attack. The leaflets were signs of the fading hopes that people's friends and loved ones might be found alive.

CHAPTER TWO

Al-Qaeda and the 9/11 Plot

Most Americans had no idea who might have launched the attacks of September 11, 2001. U.S. intelligence officers, however, immediately suspected who was behind the attacks. A radical Islamic terrorist organization named al-Qaeda had a record of threats against the United States. Its leader, the rich Saudi exile Osama bin Laden had called in 1998 for attacks on Americans. The organization had already attacked U.S. embassies and naval vessels in other parts of the world. Some agents of the Federal Bureau of Investigation (FBI) had suspected that al-Qaeda might try an attack in the United States, but they did not have any firm evidence and their superiors ignored the warnings.

Al-Qaeda—the Arabic phrase means "the base"—supports a strict form of Islam. It sees the United States and other Western countries as enemies of Islam because of their liberal social values and their economic influence. Months of investigation into the attacks confirmed that al-Qaeda was behind them.

Identifying the Culprits

Within forty-eight hours of the attacks on September 11, the FBI used seat numbers provided in the phone calls from people on the airplanes, along with booking records, to identify eighteen of the nineteen hijackers. In a hijacker's car left at Logan International Airport, Boston, investigators found a copy of the Koran—the holy book of Islam—and pilots' manuals.

▼ Osama bin Laden (left) and Ayman al-Zawahiri, the leaders of al-Qaeda, in Afghanistan in 1998.

The FBI traced the hijackers and confirmed that they had been living in the United States for several months. Some had trained to become pilots. At least four of the men had been suspected by military intelligence of belonging to al-Qaeda, but the suspicions either were not passed to security services or were not treated seriously because the men all seemed to have valid entry visas for the United States. After the attacks, the failure of agencies such as the FBI to prevent the suspected terrorists from entering the country or to detect their activities once they had arrived came in for heavy criticism.

The luggage of the man who was determined to have been the leader of the hijackers, Egyptian Mohammed Atta, had not been loaded onto Flight 11. It was held back as part of standard security procedures. The suitcase contained handwritten instructions to the hijackers that revealed the religious motivation behind the attack. Atta's Arabic notes told the hijackers to be well-dressed for their mission, to recite

Bin Laden's Letter to America

In November 2002, Osama bin Laden published a four-thousand-word "Letter to America" on the Internet as a response to the many articles published since 9/11 that asked why al-Qaeda had attacked the United States. The document is full of religious references—bin Laden quotes eight passages from the Koran and mentions Allah (God) nearly thirty times—but it also lists a wide range of political grievances against the United States. They include, for example, U.S. policy toward Palestine and Israel, where the United States supports Israel's moves to prevent Palestinian terror attacks, and toward Chechnya and Russia, where it supports the Russian government's military action against Muslim Chechens who want to establish a separate Islamic state. The document is also heavily critical of the U.S.

capitalist or free-market system and the constitutional separation of church and state. It says the separation contradicts "the pure nature which affirms Absolute Authority to the Lord and your Creator."

Bin Laden's reason for attacking Americans is that they pay the taxes that he says buy the bombs that are dropped on Islamic countries, such as during the 1991 Gulf War in Iraq or the 1986 attack on Tripoli, Libya, or attacks in August 1998 on Khartoum, Sudan, and targets in Afghanistan. In his letter, bin Laden claims that al-Qaeda targets U.S. citizens because their taxes help finance the U.S. military, and because they elect U.S. leaders who shape policies toward Muslim states. The letter also declares the superiority of Allah and urges the world to unite under Islam.

verses from the Koran to give them courage, and to think of the heavenly rewards they would receive after their deaths. It ended "We are of God, and to God we return."

The Origin of Al-Qaeda

Al-Qaeda began during a war fought in the Central Asian country of Afghanistan. The war began as a struggle by Muslim Afghans against the communist Afghan government, which was supported by the Soviet Union. Volunteers from throughout the Islamic world traveled to fight with the

Afghan Muslims, particularly after 1979, when the Soviet army entered to support the Afghan government. The war was popular among fundamentalist Muslims—those who believe in following the laws of the faith to the letter—who saw the conflict as a *jihad*, or holy war against non-Muslims.

In the 1980s Osama bin Laden went to fight in Afghanistan, but his real talent lay in organizing. He came from a wealthy Saudi Arabian family. He used his own money, as well as money he raised from other Saudis, to buy arms and send Muslims from other countries to Afghanistan. He also paid for Muslims to train as guerrilla fighters in neighboring Pakistan. After the Soviet army left Afghanistan in 1989, bin Laden wanted the network he had founded to help Muslims prepare for other conflicts around the globe. He adopted the name al-Qaeda.

Ayman Al-Zawahiri

Bin Laden also came into contact with other Islamic extremists. They included the Egyptian former surgeon Ayman al-Zawahiri. In Egypt, al-Zawahiri had founded a branch of the Islamic Jihad terrorist movement. Al-Zawahiri and Bin Laden combined their organizations, and some experts believe this larger group made Bin Laden more ambitious to launch terrorist attacks. Some observers credit al-Zawahiri with being the real leader of al-Qaeda, although he is officially bin Laden's deputy. The organization is so secretive, however, that it is difficult to know its true structure.

The Gulf War

In August 1990, Iraq invaded its oil-rich neighbor Kuwait, prompting fears that Iraqi leader Saddam Hussein was seeking to dominate oil production in the Middle East. Saudi Arabia feared it would be attacked next. Bin Laden promised to rally an army of *mujahideen* (Muslim guerrilla fighters) to drive the Iraqis from Kuwait in the same way that they had defeated the communists in Afghanistan. The Saudis, however, chose to rely for help

▲ *Mujahideen* in Afghanistan man a gun during the war against the communist government and its Soviet allies. Muslims from around the world fought in this war.

on a coalition of international forces led by the United States. Within weeks of Iraq's invasion, many thousands of mostly U.S. troops gathered in Saudi Arabia in preparation for Operation Desert Storm, the counter-invasion to drive the Iraqi army out of Kuwait.

Saudi Arabia is the site of Islam's most holy places, including the city of Mecca, which all Muslims try to visit at least once in their lives. The presence of so many non–Muslim forces in Saudi Arabia enraged many extreme Muslims, including bin Laden and fundamentalist Saudi religious leaders. They believe that the West threatens Islamic values. The presence of female military personnel in Western clothes, for example, broke strict Islamic rules that women should not work outside the home and should wear veils to preserve their modesty. Bin Laden accused Saudi leaders of abandoning Islam.

Bin Laden and the Taliban

After criticizing Saudi Arabia, bin Laden was no longer welcome in that country. In 1991, he moved to Sudan, in northeast Africa. There, he built more relationships with Islamic terrorist groups. Saudi Arabia and the United States complained to the Sudanese government that bin Laden had links with terrorism, and, in 1996, he was forced to leave. He returned to Afghanistan, where the fall of the government in 1992 had begun a civil war among various *mujahideen* groups. In 1996, an Islamist group, the Taliban ("God's students"), took power.

The Taliban shared many of bin Laden's views. Like him, they were influenced by a strict form of Islam called Wahhabism. The Taliban closed schools, banned all forms of music and dancing, and forbade women from working outside the home. The Taliban said that such restrictions were based on *sharia* law, the laws that fundamentalist Muslims believe are based on the Koran; most Muslim scholars argue that such a claim is based on a misreading of the Koran.

Jihad

Al-Qaeda was inspired by the idea of "jihad," an Arabic word that means a holy war in defense of Islam. The concept of jihad appears in the Koran, the Islamic holy book, and is mainly associated with a personal struggle against religious doubt. Eventually, however, the word also came to refer to struggles against unbelievers who threatened Islam. Islamic scholars offer a wide range of interpretations of jihad. Most continue to define it as a spiritual struggle to maintain a good Muslim life. Some more radical scholars and clerics, however, argue that the idea of jihad supports the use of war and terrorism to defend Islam; their message appeals to disaffected or impressionable Muslims who see Islamic values as being under attack by the West and particularly by the United States.

In radical interpretations of Islam, warriors who die during a jihad are martyrs and receive great rewards in heaven. Such a belief may help to explain the rise of Islamic terrorists of who are willing to die for their cause, like the 9/11 hijackers or other suicide bombers. In 1998, Osama bin Laden claimed the authority to declare a fatwa—a decree usually issued by an Islamic religious leader—claiming that all Americans are legitimate targets of a jihad.

Sharing bin Laden's extreme hostility toward the West, and particularly the United States, the Taliban offered him a safe base and the chance to train potential terrorists and raise money for terrorism. In 1998, bin Laden and other al-Qaeda leaders, including al-Zawahiri, declared a fatwa, against the United States. Because a fatwa is usually issued by an Islamic religious leader, bin Laden did not strictly have the authority to declare one. In his fatwa, he claimed in that it was the duty of Muslims to kill U.S. citizens.

Some time afterward, bin Laden met an important ally, the Kuwaiti Khalid Sheikh Mohammed. Sheikh Mohammed's nephew, Ramzi Yousef, had been involved in a 1993 bombing of the World Trade Center. Sheikh Mohammed himself had plotted in 1995 to blow up U.S. airliners over the Pacific Ocean. The plan was foiled when police officers discovered details of it on a computer during a separate investigation.

Sheikh Mohammed saw that it would be possible to use an airliner as a flying bomb. He came up with a plan to fly up to nine airliners into U.S. targets. Bin Laden agreed to finance what

became known as the "planes operation." The two men and an associate, Mohammed Atef, made a list of possible targets. It included the Pentagon, the White House, the Capitol, and the World Trade Center.

Assembling the Attackers

Sheikh Mohammed was responsible for planning the operation. He recruited al-Qaeda members to train to become pilots. Two of the initial recruits, the Saudis Khalid al-Midhar and Nawaf al-Hazmi, did eventually take part in the 9/11 attacks, although not as pilots. The pair trained on flight simulators in Pakistan, but when they moved to the United States in January 2000 to carry

▼ The spreading of Western businesses, such as KFC, into Saudi Arabia enrages Islamists, who see the West as a threat to what they interpret as the values of Islam.

on their flying lessons in Los Angeles, their poor English forced them to give up their training. Sheikh Mohammed needed new recruits.

New Recruits

Meanwhile, four young Muslims arrived in Kandahar, Afghanistan, a major center for al-Qaeda. They had met as students in Hamburg, Germany, and had been drawn together by their Islamist beliefs. They were Mohamed Atta, from Egypt, who is said to have been a member of al-Zawahiri's terrorist group; Marwan al Shehhi, from the United Arab Emirates; Ziad Jarrah, from Lebanon; and Ramzi Binalshibh, from Yemen. The four wanted to join Muslims in Chechnya, in southern Russia, fighting for independence from Russia. When it was discovered that the four men spoke English, they were recruited for the planes operation instead. Mohamed Atta took charge of the preparations.

Atta decided that U.S. flight schools were the best place to learn how to pilot an airliner. Three of the four men got U.S. visas by using false passports, but Binalshibh was turned down. In his place, a Saudi named Hani Hanjour was recruited to fly the fourth airplane. He was a qualified pilot, so he did not join the other three at flying school.

In the United States, the al-Qaeda operatives lived quietly, without drawing attention to themselves. They were not monitored by security agencies. They had some interaction with local Muslims and made trips abroad and in the eastern United States.

Another al-Qaeda member arrived in the United States in January 2001. He was a French citizen named Zacarias Moussaoui, originally from Morocco. Instructors at his flying school in Minnesota were suspicious that Moussaoui was only interested in learning about some parts of how to fly an airplane. When authorities investigated Moussaoui in August 2001, he was arrested on immigration charges. He was in jail when the 9/11 attacks took place. Moussaoui denied any role in the attacks—although he admitted being a member of al-Qaeda—but many people believe that he was intended to be among the hijackers on 9/11.

Final Preparations

In addition to the actual pilots, other terrorists were recruited to provide the force to take over the aircraft. These terrorists—some of whom may not realized that they were taking part in a suicide mission—arrived in the United States between April and June 2001. Meanwhile, Atta and his fellow pilots made frequent cross-country flights to discover the best time to begin the attack and to test ways to smuggle weapons onto the planes. Atta informed the al-Qaeda leadership that the attack was set for September 11; between August 25 and September 5, the hijackers bought their tickets.

The source of some facts now known about the planning of the 9/11 attacks is Ramzi Binalshibh, who was originally intended to be one of the hijackers. He was captured in Pakistan in September 2002. Before his arrest, Binalshibh told the Arabic-language TV station al-Jazeera how he traveled to Kandahar to meet the leaders of the operation. The suspected mastermind of the plot, Kahlid Sheikh Mohammed, was arrested in Pakistan in March 2003; it is hoped that he will provide important information about not only the 9/11 attacks on New York and Washington, D. C., but also a bombing in Bali, Indonesia, in 2002 and the suicide bombing of a Tunisian synagogue in the same year.

▲ Mohamed Atta (right) prepares to board a plane in Portland, Maine, early on September 11, 2001. That plane flew to Boston, where Atta boarded American Airlines Flight 11.

Muslims in the United States

Around four million Muslims live in the United States, the overwhelming majority of whom utterly condemn Islamist terrorism, especially the 9/11 attacks. About 60 percent of U.S. Muslims are from families who emigrated from other countries, mainly in the Middle East and Africa; the remainder are linked to the African American Nation of Islam, a religious group. Many live in California and New York, but it is difficult to generalize about a Muslim community.

The religion does not have a single rigid organization, and it has many different denominations. A Muslim might attend mosque regularly and follow the basic precepts of prayer and charity, but he or she might not follow dietary rules strictly or expect women to cover even their hair when out of doors. On the other hand, some Muslims follow the rules of the religion to the letter.

After the attacks on September 11, 2001, verbal and physical abuse of Muslims and mosques in the United States increased markedly, as a tiny minority of Americans held all believers responsible for the actions of the terrorists. Many politicians, including President George W. Bush, condemned such reactions. They emphasized the long tradition of peace and tolerance among Muslims in the United States and the contribution they make to the country's prosperity.

CHAPTER THREE

Islamist Terrorism

Osama bin Laden and other Islamist terrorists claim that the basis for their actions lies in the teachings of Islam. Very few Muslims agree. The vast majority of the more than one billion Muslims in the world condemn all forms of terrorism. For them, Islam is a peaceful and tolerant religion. However, there is also a long tradition of radical Islam intent on creating nations governed by Islamic clerics and ruled by Islamic *sharia* law. The supporters of such ambitions sometimes sympathize with the terrorists' aims. After bombings in London in July 2005, for example, the Islamic cleric Omar Bahkri Mohammed, who was living in the city, provoked anger in an interview with journalists. He said that, even if he knew that terrorists were planning an attack, he would not tell the police. A Muslim, he argued, should never report another Muslim to the police. Again, this view is held by only a tiny minority of Muslims.

What Is Islam?

Islam is one of the world's three great monotheistic religions, along with Christianity and Judaism. Like them, it originated in the Middle East. In 610 C.E., the Prophet Muhammad (c.570–632) began preaching in the Arabian Peninsula, saying that his message was given to him by God's angel, Gabriel. His message was recorded in the Muslim holy book, the Koran, which was written in Arabic. Many people in Arabia accepted Muhammad as their spiritual leader and adopted his faith, Islam. ("Islam" is an Arabic word meaning "submission" to the will of God.) After the Prophet's death, a dispute about

▼ Rescue workers carry away the body of one of the two hundred victims of a bomb blast in a Bali nightclub in October 2002. The Islamist terrorist group Jemaah Islamiyah carried out the attack, which is thought to have been planned by the al-Qaeda leader Khalid Sheikh Mohammed.

who should succeed him split the faith into Sunni and Shia branches; the divide remains a problem today.

History of Political Islam

After Muhammad's death, Islam spread throughout the Middle East and North Africa and into Spain. Its spiritual message and code for living found many followers. During the centuries that followed, a succession of Islamic empires dominated the Middle East and Central Asia, including the Turkish Ottoman Empire, which was not Arab. This empire fell at the end of World War I (1914–1918). During the war, the Arabs within the empire launched a guerrilla war against their Turkish rulers with support from France and Britain. After the war, despite Arab hopes of independence, the British and French split much of the Middle East between them. They governed it as a number of territories called mandates or protectorates.

In the mandate of Palestine, the British allowed the free immigration of Jewish settlers into an area in which most of the population were Arab, but which had been home to ancient Jewish kingdoms. The British had declared in 1917 their support for the eventual creation of a Jewish state in part of the region.

Wahhabism

Muhammad ibn Abd al-Wahhab (1703–1792) was an eighteenth-century Arabian scholar who thought that Islam had moved too far away from the faith preached by the Prophet Muhammad. He called for a purification of Islam, and because of his radical views he was forced to leave his home in the Hejaz, a region on the west coast of the Arabian Peninsula in what is now Saudi Arabia. He took refuge with Muhammad bin Saud, the founder of the Saudi dynasty. Wahhab and his disciples interpreted the Koran literally. They banned all pictures (and later photographs), singing, and musical instruments, and did not celebrate the Prophet's birthday, unlike many other Muslims.

After the Saudi conquest of the Hejaz in 1926, Wahhab's disciples received extensive support from the government. It gave them money to pay for schools and missionary activities in Arabia and elsewhere. The schools have been especially influential in Pakistan, where a military government in the late 1970s encouraged a strict form of Islam and the application of Islamic law. The Taliban, who ruled Afghanistan from 1996 to 2001, were also greatly influenced by Wahhabism. Within Saudi Arabia, Wahhabis are among those who most loudly protest the corrupting influence of the West on the country.

Arabia, meanwhile, became an independent kingdom that occupied most of the Arabian Peninsula. In 1926, the Saudi family came to the throne of what later became known as Saudi Arabia. They followed a strict version of Islam known as Wahhabism.

The Rise of Radical Islam

Arabs living under European mandates formed political groups to work for independence. Some of these groups were pan–Arab, inspired more by their common Arabic cultural heritage and language than by their shared religion; some even wanted to create a single Arab nation. Other groups believed that the main unifying force in the region should be Islam.

The first example of such an Islamist group was the Muslim Brotherhood, founded in Egypt in 1928. It quickly became influential throughout the Middle East. In the 1970s, an organization that broke away from the Muslim Brotherhood, Egyptian Islamic Jihad, would become one of the most deadly of Islamist terrorist groups.

The French and British withdrew from the Middle East after World War II (1939–1945). Their departure brought increased influence from the United States, which was drawn to the region by its vast reserves of oil.

The State of Israel

After the Holocaust of World War II, in which millions of Jews were murdered by the Nazis, Jewish immigration to Palestine increased. In November 1947, the United Nations approved a partition plan for the region of Palestine that intended to create both a Jewish state and a Palestinian Arab state. Britain declared that its mandate over the region would end in May 1948. Fighting between Jews and Arabs broke out in the region following the

The Muslim Brotherhood

The first Islamist group, the Muslim Brotherhood, was formed in British-ruled Egypt in 1928. During the 1930s, it spread to Syria, Palestine, and Transjordan (now Jordan). It was at first a movement for social reform, but became a political group in 1939. It opposes the separation of religion from public administration and rejects Western consumer values. A key thinker behind the Muslim Brotherhood was the Egyptian Sayyid Qutb (1906–1966). He argued that the United States was Islam's most dangerous opponent, because its values contradicted those of Islam and its military and economic strength made it highly influential.

The Muslim Brotherhood had close ties to a military group in Egypt known as the Free Officers Movement, which overthrew the Egyptian monarchy in 1952. The Free Officers, however, was inspired in part by European socialist ideals, which the Brotherhood rejected. In 1954, the Brotherhood was implicated in an assassination plot against Egyptian leader Colonel Gamel Abdel Nasser, and many of it members were imprisoned, including Qutb. In 1966, Qutb was hanged after another alleged assassination plot against Nasser.

Members of the Brotherhood have been involved in numerous terrorist attacks, especially in Syria, where it tried to overthrow the government in 1982. At the same time, they have participated in free elections in those Arab states where their organization is not banned.

announcement of the partition plan. When Israel declared independence in May 1948, it was immediately attacked by a group of Arab nations, including Egypt, Syria, Lebanon, and Iraq. After Israel's victory in late 1948, the land intended for a Palestinian Arab state was divided among Israel, Egypt, and Jordan.

The Muslim Brotherhood saw the defeat of the Arab nations in 1949 as a disaster, for which they blamed the Arab governments. Their response was to turn to violence. In Egypt, they tried to assassinate the prime minister; they also made an alliance with disgruntled army officers, who seized power in a coup in 1952. The Brotherhood hoped that the coup would bring a greater role for Islam in the country's government. Instead, Egypt's new rulers looked to allies such as the United States and the Soviet Union for support. In 1954, the Brotherhood again tried to kill an Egyptian leader, this time the nationalist prime minister Gamal Abdel Nasser (1918–1970). Nasser, who became president in 1956, foiled the plot and jailed the group's leaders. Meanwhile nationalist army officers seized power in Syria and Iraq. Throughout the Arab world, secular leaders who believed that religion and goverment should largely be kept separate were gaining power at the expense of the Islamists.

Rising Tensions

Islamists like the members of the Muslim Brotherhood believed that the secular Arab states of Egypt, Syria, and Iraq had abandoned the rules of Islam. They thought that the defeat of these nations by Israel after they attacked it again in 1967 was a judgment from God on the way the Arab states had abandoned true Islam. During the 1967 Arab-Israeli war, Israel occupied the parts of Palestine it did not already control.

▼ Chairs lay scattered and overturned in the aftermath of the assassination of Egyptian President Anwar Sadat in Cairo on October 6, 1981. Members of Egyptian Islamic Jihad opened fire on Sadat with machine guns.

The reaction of the rest of the world to the Israeli occupation angered even some moderate Muslims. The United Nations did not make the Israelis withdraw, while the United States shifted from a position of neutrality to one of strong support for Israel. Radical Muslims argued that the Arabs had to defeat Israel by whatever means they could in order to return the Palestinian Arabs to what they claim is their rightful home. They also believed that only a renewed and strict form of Islam could provide the spiritual energy to support such a long and hard struggle.

Influence of Wahhabism

In the secular Arab states, the revival of a more fundamentalist form of Islam was a cause for concern. The Egyptian government kept close watch on the Muslim Brotherhood in the late 1960s and 1970s. Many of the groups members moved to Saudi Arabia, where they found support among followers of Wahhabism. The two groups set up schools to train clerics, through the teaching of whom the Muslim Brotherhood gained new influence in the Arab world. The strict teachings of Wahhabism would inspire future Islamists to believe that attacks on non-Muslims were justified. The leaders of al-Qaeda and many of the 9/11 attackers followed Wahhabism.

Al-Zawahiri's Terrorism

Within Egypt, the Muslim Brotherhood turned away from violence during the 1980s and called for democratic elections and social reform. Some of its members, however, still believed that political assassination and attacks on the government were the only way to realize their goals. They formed a new terrorist group, Egyptian Islamic Jihad. In 1981, they assassinated Nasser's successor as president, Anwar el-Sadat (1918–1981), who had signed a treaty recognizing Israel's right to exist in 1978.

Ten years later, the same group, now led by Ayman al-Zawahiri, who later made an alliance with al-Qaeda, launched a decade-long campaign of terror to overthrow Sadat's successor as Egyptian president, Hosni Mubarak

▼ Protestors in the Iranian capital, Tehran, in 1979 display posters of Ayatollah Khomeini (left) and the "three devils": Israeli prime minister Menachem Begin, President Sadat of Egypt, and U.S. president Jimmy Carter.

(born 1929). More than a thousand people died in a series of terrorist attacks by Islamist groups including Egyptian Islamic Jihad, but the Egyptian government also killed or imprisoned many of the terrorists. Al-Zawahiri is thought to be responsible for an attack in which several dozen tourists died at the tourist site of Luxor in 1997. Although he fled the country, an Egyptian court sentenced him to death in his absence.

Militancy in Iran

While Islamist terrorists fought unsuccessfully for control of Egypt, the most powerful Arab state, men with similar views took power in a non-Arab state, Iran. In January 1979, a revolution drove out the ruling monarch, the Shah, and set up an Islamic republic under the religious leader Ayatollah Ruholla Khomeini

(1900–1989). Khomeini and his associates were uncompromising opponents of Israel. Khomeini also called the United States "the Great Satan," and blamed it for the fact that Islam did not have any influence on many Middle Eastern governments. Khomeini's anger toward America was made worse by the fact that the United States had been a close ally of the Shah.

This first success by an Islamist political movement in the Middle East alarmed the leaders of Iran's more secular neighbors: Saudi Arabia, Iraq, Kuwait, and the other Gulf states. Leaders of those states, and a number of Western powers, encouraged the secular dictator of Iraq, the Saddam Hussein (born 1937), to attack Iran in 1980. The resulting war claimed around 1.5 million lives and lasted until 1988.

Palestinian Terrorism

Khomeini proved Israel's most active Middle Eastern opponent. He saw Israel as the West's means to influence the region and combat Islam. He saw the conflict between Israel and the Palestinians not as a struggle between Jews and Arabs—he was not an Arab himself—but as a conflict between Jews and Muslims.

In 1982, the Israelis had invaded Lebanon and expelled the Palestinian Liberation Organization (PLO), the main political opposition to Israel, which was also suspected of organizing terrorist attacks. In its place, the Iranians funded a group of Lebanese Muslims to fight Israel. The new group was named Hezbollah, or "Party of God." Today, the U.S. government classifies Hezbollah as a terrorist group, but many Shia Lebanese and Palestinians see it as a political party that aims to create an exclusively Islamic state in Lebanon, destroy Israel, and impose Islamic rule in the region of Palestine.

> **Palestinian Islamic Jihad opposes both the state of Israel, which it seeks to destroy, and the secular PLO**

Hezbollah and Islamic Jihad

Hezbollah waged a guerrilla war against the Israeli occupation of southern Lebanon. It kidnapped several Americans and Europeans and launched missile attacks on northern Israel. It also staged larger attacks. In 1992, for example, a car bomb attack on Israel's embassy in Argentina killed 29 and wounded more than 100.

In 2000, Israel finally withdrew its last troops from Lebanon. The prominent role of Hezbollah in the resistance to the occupation raised the prestige of Islamists throughout the Arab world.

While Iran lent support to Lebanese Muslims, members of Egyptian Islamic Jihad helped form Palestinian Islamic Jihad. Palestinian Islamic Jihad opposes both the state of Israel, which it seeks

Arab–Israeli Conflict, 1917–1970

One of the causes that Islamists often use as an reason for terrorism is the conflict between Arabs and Jews over the state of Israel. Islamists believe that Israel occupies land that rightfully belongs to Muslims.

In 1917, the British government offered its support for the creation of a Jewish state in Palestine. At the time, about 60,000 Jews and about 600,000 Palestinian Arabs lived in the area. By the late 1940s, the Jewish population had risen to 600,000 but was still only half the number of Arabs. The United Nations divided Palestine into two states, one Arab, one Jewish. However, Arab states in the region attacked Israel as soon as it became independent in 1948; a year later, they had all been defeated.

The Arab defeat left most of Palestine under Israeli control. The rest was occupied by Israel during a second Arab-Israeli war in 1967. The United Nations ordered Israel to return the areas to Arab control, but Israel refused until the Arab countries accepted its right to exist.

Hundreds of thousands of Palestinian Arabs settled in refugee camps. Some new groups dedicated to overthrowing Israel arose in these camps. One of the most active was the Popular Front for the Liberation of Palestine (PFLP). In 1970, the PFLP hijacked three airliners and exchanged several hundred hostages for four PFLP guerrillas in European jails. Today, the secular PFLP has been sidelined by Islamist groups in their struggle against Israel.

▶ The PFLP blew up three airliners on September 12, 1970, at Dawson's Field, Jordan. The planes had been hijacked and flown to the airstrip a week earlier. The passengers and crew were released before the explosions.

World Trade Center Attack, 1993

On February 26, 1993, a bomb hidden in a truck exploded in an underground parking garage of the World Trade Center in New York City. Six people were killed and more than a thousand were wounded by the blast. The FBI learned that the truck had been rented by a man named Mohammad Salameh, a Palestinian living in the United States. Salameh and two other Muslim extremists linked to the bombing were arrested.

Eventually, the FBI investigation led to Sheikh Omar Abdel-Rahman, an Egyptian cleric who had arrived in the United States in 1990. Like other Islamists, Sheikh Omar believed that the United States was the enemy of all Muslims. He openly preached his message that U.S. society violated Islamic laws from a mosque in Brooklyn.

A fifth plotter, Ramzi Yousef, left the country almost immediately after the bombing. He was not caught until January 1995 in the Philippines, where he was plotting the hijacking of several U.S. airliners with his uncle, Khalid Sheikh Mohammed. Yousef and another terrorist arrested in 1993, Ahmad Ajaj, had links with a training camp in Afghanistan. The 1993 attack on the World Trade Center was the first act of Islamist terrorism on U.S. soil. In its links with Islamic extremism and wartorn Afghanistan, it also offered a precursor to the attacks of 9/11.

hundreds of Israeli lives, but some of its claims may be for attacks by other Palestinian terror organizations.

The Intifada and Hamas

In 1987, Palestinians living in the West Bank and Gaza Strip—Arab-dominated areas occupied by Israel in 1967—began attacking Israeli soldiers and police. The uprising, known as the intifada, a term meaning "shaking off," saw the emergence of a new group to rival the PLO for the political leadership of the Palestinians. Hamas, or the "Islamic Resistance Movement," grew out of the Muslim Brotherhood in Palestine in 1987, and originally emphasized social activities in the deprived Palestinian areas. Politically, however, it insisted that the territory on which Israel stands was given by God to the Muslims, and that no part of it could be given up.

Concessions and Resistance

In 1988, the PLO recognized Israel's right to exist. In contrast, Hamas and Islamic Jihad insisted that Islamists were obliged to claim back Israeli territory, expel the Jews, and create an Islamic state in the region.

The PLO's concession was welcome to Western governments. In return, the United States encouraged Israel to work with the PLO to create the Palestinian Authority, an organization that would have some political power in the Gaza Strip and the West Bank, although these areas remained under Israeli occupation, and would act as the

to destroy, and the secular PLO. Since 1986, it has launched grenade attacks and suicide bombings within Israel. Islamic Jihad claims credit for many attacks, such as suicide bombings on buses in Jerusalem, that have taken

Targeting Americans

Throughout the 1980s, while parts of the Middle East were in often violent turmoil, Islamist terrorists launched attacks against the United States in the region to protest its presence and particularly its financial and political support for Israel. One such attack came in October 1983, when a suicide bomber who likely belonged to Hezbollah drove a truck packed with explosives into a U.S. Marine Corps barracks in Beirut, Lebanon. The attack killed 241 U.S. soldiers who were part of a multinational force trying to restore order to Lebanon.

Attacks on U.S. targets intensified after the 1990–1991 Gulf War to liberate Kuwait from Saddam Hussein. To prevent Iraq from destabilizing the area again, many U.S. forces remained in the region after the war. In November 1995, a car bomb exploded outside a joint Saudi-U.S. training base in Saudi Arabia. A similar attack at

representative of Palestinians abroad. Under a 1993 agreement, which also ended the intifada, PLO leader Yasser Arafat became chairman of the Palestinian Authority. He pledged to punish Palestinians who carried out terrorist attacks on Israel, including members of Hezbollah and Hamas. The reaction of those groups to the agreement was to increase their campaign of suicide bombings. Arafat and the PLO soon found that support for the Palestinian Islamist terrorists came from beyond their control. The main sources of their support were states dedicated to the destruction of Israel, such as Iran, Syria, Libya, and Iraq. The PLO could not deliver on its promise of peace.

▼ The USS *Cole* was anchored off Yemen in October 2000, when a suicide-bomb attack ripped a large hole in the ship's hull. The attack, which was carried out by al-Qaeda, killed seventeen sailors.

Dharhan, Saudi Arabia, in June 1996 killed nineteen U.S. Air Force personnel and wounded nearly four hundred. Islamists also made their first attack on Americans at home. In 1993, a truck bomb exploded in a garage of the World Trade Center.

In February 1998, al-Zawahiri, now a fugitive in Pakistan, merged his Islamic Jihad organization with bin Laden's al-Qaeda. In August that year, al-Qaeda's first real terrorist attack came. Two truck bombs were driven at the same time into the U.S. embassies in Dar es Salaam, Tanzania, and Nairobi, Kenya. A total of twelve Americans and 212 African embassy workers died in the explosions. In October 2000, two al-Qaeda suicide bombers used a small boat to explode a bomb against the side of the warship USS *Cole* in the port of Aden, Yemen, killing seventeen sailors.

Continuing Attacks

Since the attacks of September 11, 2001, militant Islamist terrorism has continued. In October 2002, more than two hundred people died in the bombing of a popular tourist nightclub in Bali, Indonesia, carried out by Jemaah Islamiyah, a group thought to have links to al-Qaeda. Indonesia is a mainly Muslim nation but has close connections with the West; Islamists want to make it a strict Islamic state.

In 1993, a truck bomb exploded in a garage of the World Trade Center in New York City

In 2003, the United States and its allies, including Great Britain and Spain, invaded Iraq. They overthrew the regime of Saddam Hussein and occupied Iraq. On March 11, 2004, four commuter trains traveling into Madrid, Spain, during the morning rush hour were blown up by a group of Islamist terrorists from Morocco. It is thought that the bombs were detonated by cell phone. More than 200 people died in the blasts and around 1,400 were wounded. The terrorists' attack was a protest against Western influence in the Muslim world. On July 7, 2005, four suicide bombers blew themselves up on subway trains and a bus in London, England, killing 51 people. Many observers saw the attacks in Madrid and London as a result of Spanish and British support for the war in Iraq.

Other Groups

Beside al-Qaeda, Islamist terrorist groups operating at the start of the twenty-first century included the Algerian-based Islamic Salvation Front (FIS) and the Pakistan-Kashmir-based Harakatul Ansar (HUA). A fundamentalist political party in Algeria, FIS is believed to support groups that have been implicated in major attacks such as the 1994 hijacking of an airliner belonging to Air France, the French national airline.

In Pakistan, HUA, like al-Qaeda, began by fighting against the Soviets in Afghanistan during the 1980s. It operates mostly in Kashmir, a province whose control is disputed between largely Muslim Pakistan and mostly Hindu India, where it launches attacks on non-Muslims. HUA is thought to draw wide support from across the Muslim world.

Islamist Goals

Although Islamist terrorists claim religion as the main justification for their crimes, they often have other motives. Many have a political goal, such as a change in government policy. Much Islamist terrorism is carried out against other Muslims, including supporters of governments that the terrorists believe are not following true Islamic values. Islamists in Iraq, for example, have murdered Iraqis serving in the new, post-Saddam government and have kidnapped and killed officials from Saudi Arabia and other Islamic countries. In some cases, the terrorists try to divide a country and establish an independent Islamic state. In all cases, however, Islamist terrorists blame other countries, particularly the United States, for the problems that Muslims face around the world.

▼ The mangled remains of a commuter train destroyed by a bomb in Madrid, Spain, on March 11, 2004. Islamist terrorists from Morocco were to blame for the attack.

CHAPTER FOUR

Facing the Islamists

On September 20, 2001, President George W. Bush addressed a joint session of Congress. It was nine days after the attacks in New York City and Washington, D.C., and the total number of deaths was still not known. In his speech, Bush described the attacks as "an act of war against our country." The president blamed Osama bin Laden and his Islamist organization, then based in Afghanistan, for the attacks. He said that the United States was now at war with al-Qaeda.

U.S. Response to 9/11

The president demanded that the Islamist Taliban government of Afghanistan hand over Osama bin Laden for trial in the United States. If they failed, the United States would invade. The Taliban refused.

On October 7, 2001, U.S. armed forces and a wide international coalition launched Operation Enduring Freedom, a military attack intended to destroy al-Qaeda camps in Afghanistan and capture al-Qaeda members. Air strikes destroyed Taliban defenses, while U.S. special forces entered Afghanistan to assist the Northern Alliance, a group of local warlords who were eager to overthrow the Taliban. U.S. ground troops followed in November, fighting Taliban and al-Qaeda forces. They captured many suspected al-Qaeda members and destroyed their bases; the Taliban government was toppled. In Afghanistan's mountainous terrain, however, bin Laden and other al-Qaeda leaders escaped.

In other parts of Enduring Freedom, U.S. military forces were sent to Djibouti, in northeast Africa, and to the Philippines in the Pacific. From Djibouti, they

▼ The wreckage of a double-decker bus stands in a London street after a rush-hour bomb attack on July 7, 2005. The blast was one of four in a coordinated attack by suicide bombers on the city's transportation system.

struck at suspected al-Qaeda terrorists in Yemen and Somalia, while U.S. forces aided the Philippine government in its long conflict against Islamist guerrillas.

Military action was not the only U.S. response to the attacks. In announcing what he called the "war on terror," President Bush said that the CIA and special forces would engage in covert operations that would remain "secret even in success." Agents would also trace and cut off the funding on which terrorist groups relied.

The U.S. government realized that its effort had to be on an international scale to succeed, so it pressed other countries, such as Indonesia, to take action against terrorists within their borders, including Islamists. Bush also warned that the struggle might extend to states that supported terrorist groups, such as Iraq, Iran, and North Korea. He said, "Our war on terrorism begins with al-Qaeda, but it does not end there. It will not end until every terrorist group of global reach has been found, stopped, and defeated."

A Failure of Intelligence?

At home, meanwhile, an investigation began into how the attacks had

Security at Home

The War on Terror has had a noticeable impact on daily life for many Americans. The year after the 9/11 attacks in 2001, the Bush administration formed the Department of Homeland Security to coordinate the defense of U. S. borders. One of the department's roles is to issue a regularly updated color-coded risk advisory that shows how likely it believes a terrorist attack to be.

Because the 9/11 attacks used airplanes, meanwhile, security at airports was increased. More restrictive parking rules were set up, and passengers and their luggage were subjected to more intensive searches. More police officers and even soldiers were used to guard airports. Armed federal officers now fly regularly on aircraft, where cockpit doors have to be fitted with security locks.

In the weeks following the 9/11 attacks, a series of incidents caused widespread apprehension regarding the mail. A few days after 9/11, several letters were sent to lawmakers and news media that were contaminated with anthrax, a bacterium that causes a disease that affects the skin and breathing. Five people died from the disease, and twenty-two others suffered some level of anthrax infection.

Throughout the country, mail facilities, government offices, and other businesses were placed on a high state of alert. At first, the letters were thought to be linked to the 9/11 attacks, and up to twelve hundred foreign nationals, almost all of Arab or Muslim background, were detained. Although the anthrax attack has never been fully explained, it is now believed that it was unrelated to 9/11.

happened and whether they could have been prevented. The main body responsible for the inquiry was the National Commission on Terrorist Attacks Upon the United States, which was set up by Congress and the president in 2002.

The Commission confirmed that the security services were aware of the threat posed by Osama bin Laden well before September 2001. Al-Qaeda had been monitored by the Central Intelligence Agency (CIA), while the FBI had acquired the names of people thought to be al-Qaeda terrorists. President Bill Clinton had even authorized the assassination of bin Laden, although the operation was not carried out.

In June 2005, Congressman Curt Weldon of Pennsylvania claimed that a secret military intelligence unit had identified Mohammed Atta and three other hijackers as members of an al-Qaeda cell a year before the attacks. Weldon's claim was not officially confirmed, but the investigation into the 9/11 attacks had already confirmed that two of the four hijackers had been tracked on their way to the United States. It also found that warnings about their presence in the United States had not been acted upon.

Warning Signs

The director of the CIA, George Tenet, told the Commission that in summer 2001 "the system was blinking red," meaning that there were signs that something might happen. Reports

about possible attacks using aircraft even reached the White House. National security advisor Condoleezza Rice said in May 2002, however, that they gave no specific information. They could not have stopped an attack without closing down all flights in the nation. No one imagined such drastic action was needed. Rice said: "I don't think that anybody could have predicted that these people would take an airplane and slam it into the World Trade Center, take another one and slam it into the Pentagon."

The Patriot Act

The military action after the September 11 attacks was matched by measures to increase security at home. In October 2001, President Bush signed into law the Patriot Act. The act allowed intelligence and police officers to share more information and gave them more power to monitor

▲ Federal agents undergo disinfection after investigating a package suspected of being contaminated with anthrax in October 2001.

telephone conversations and e-mails, if approved by a judge. The Patriot Act also allowed the Immigration and Naturalization Service (INS), which administers the entry and exit of foreigners to and from the United States, to detain non-American citizens for up to seven days without charging them with a crime. The act also widened the kind of activities that would allow the government to define an organization a terrorist group.

Other parts of the act allowed federal agents to enter homes and search for evidence of terrorist activity without informing suspects. Such searches, like other provisions in the act, had to be authorized by a judge before they took place. The act also allowed prosecutors to use evidence in court that was kept secret from defendants accused of terrorism.

The government argued that the measures in the Patriot Act are essential to combat terrorism inside the United States. Many Americans agreed. Many others, however, were concerned that the act threatened civil liberties such as the right to privacy and the right to free speech. They thought it gave the government too much power to interfere in peoples' lives and to monitor its political opponents.

In 2002, the government created a Department of Homeland Security. One of the jobs of the department is the prevention of terrorism against the

country. It brought together twenty-two existing agencies, with around 170,000 employees and a budget of about $40 billion. President Bush announced, "Creating a new Department of Homeland Security will ensure that our efforts to defend this country are comprehensive and united." Critics of the reorganization argued that it did not affect either of the agencies that were most widely blamed for the failings that may have allowed the 9/11 attacks, the CIA and the FBI.

Attacking al-Qaeda

Despite the war in Afghanistan and the new national security measures, the threat of further attacks remained. Major leaders of al-Qaeda, including Osama bin Laden and Ayman al-Zawahiri, managed to avoid capture.

▼ A protestor wears a gag to show the effect he believes the Patriot Act will have on free speech in the United States.

Could the Attacks Have Been Prevented?

Since the attacks of September 11, 2001, debate has continued about whether they could have been prevented. It was one of the questions considered by the National Commission on Terrorist Attacks Upon the United States.

The commission concluded that the attacks were the result of a failure of U.S defenses on four levels. They called the first a failure of imagination. Before 9/11, al-Qaeda had killed fewer than fifty Americans. No one had imagined that it could mount an attack on such a scale as the events of 9/11.

The second failure was one of policy. In the aftermath of the first al-Qaeda attacks on U.S. targets on U.S. embassies and the USS *Cole*, the United States did not know how to respond to an opponent like Osama bin Laden, who was based out of reach in Afghanistan and had no specific demands.

The commission said that the third failure was one of capabilities. Before 9/11, the United States tried to meet the threat from al-Qaeda with the same institutions on which it had relied during the Cold War. The CIA, which monitored al-Qaeda operations in Afghanistan, did not have the capacity to take action against it there. The Department of Defense, which controlled U.S. military forces, was not involved in the operation.

The final failure was one of management. Security agencies missed chances to stop the plot or arrest the plotters, partly because there was no coordination among them. The CIA and the FBI, in particular, did not share information about the movements of suspected terrorists who were later involved in the 9/11 attacks. The intelligence insitutions themselves were poorly managed. When George Tenet sent a memo to his officials in December 1998 that read, "We are at war. I want no resources or people spared in this effort," his priorities were not followed through by CIA officers.

Despite identifying numerous failings in the security services, the Commission did not come to a clear conclusion about whether the attacks of September 11 were preventable. It argued that the plot might have been nipped in the bud. It also said, however, "Since the plotters were flexible and resourceful, we cannot know whether any single step or series of steps would have defeated them."

In the summer of 2003, a congressional committee echoed the findings of the Commission. It said that the FBI had missed opportunities to break up the plot. The Bureau ignored, for example, reports from one of its own agents about two of the eventual hijackers living in San Diego with an FBI informant. The CIA delayed telling the FBI that these men were suspected terrorists. When the FBI eventually found out, it did not circulate the information to its offices, including the one in San Diego.

The Terrorists' Mouthpiece?

The first sight most Americans had of Osama bin Laden came soon after the 9/11 attacks, when news shows aired clips from Arabic-language TV station Al Jazeera ("the Island"), which is based in the Persian Gulf state of Qatar. Al Jazeera's video showed bin Laden claiming credit for the attacks. Another tape broadcast on the station showed one of the 9/11 hijackers reading out his will.

Al Jazeera soon became notorious in the West for airing videos or audio tapes of bin Laden and other terrorists. The station says that it is simply reporting the news from a Muslim point of view. It points out that its Muslim viewers complain when it shows, say,

Israeli officials defending Israel's policies. All the same, the station has become the Islamists' favored means of spreading their views or boasting of their actions.

This has led to Al Jazeera being criticized for anti-Western bias. The U.S. government slammed its coverage of the 2003 invasion of Iraq, when Al Jazeera broadcast images of U.S. prisoners of war. The network said that it was echoing western stations that broadcast images of Iraqi prisoners.

▼ In 2002, CNN aired a clip shown on Al Jazeera of a message from Ahmed al-Ghamdi, one of the 9/11 hijackers.

Many experts think that they escaped over the border to Pakistan, where Islamists have many sympathizers. They may still be in the country. The government of Pakistan, however, is an ally of the United States in the war on terror. Its security forces have successfully arrested some leading members of al-Qaeda since the war, including Khalid Sheik Mohammed and Ramzi Binalshibh. According to Pakistan's president Pervez Musharraf, Osama bin Laden himself came close to being captured in early summer 2004 but again escaped.

Bin Laden and al-Zawahiri, meanwhile, have regularly issued video or audio tape messages. They contain praise for the September 11 attackers and threats to the U.S. and other governments, including those of Arab states that bin Laden believes have abandoned the true interpretation of the Islamic faith.

The Shoe Bomber

Al-Qaeda has attempted many terrorist attacks since September 2001. In December of that same year, a British-born Muslim named Richard Reid was arrested after trying to blow up an airliner flying from Paris, France, to Miami. Reid tried to detonate explosives hidden in his shoe. The explosion would have blown a hole in the airplane that would have caused it to crash in the Atlantic. Passengers and crew members overpowered Reid when they saw him trying to light a fuse connected to the explosives.

The FBI Under Fire

One of the targets of the harshest criticism after the attacks of 9/11 was the Federal Bureau of Investigation (FBI). The FBI was widely criticized for its failure to share information with other security agencies and even among different parts of its own organization. Poor communications between its field offices and its headquarters in Washington, D.C., had also prevented suspicions about some of the 9/11 hijackers from being acted upon. Some critics say that such communication failures have been typical of the FBI since it was established in the 1920s.

In November 2001, Attorney General John Ashcroft announced a reorganization of the FBI to enable it to fight terrorism more effectively. The plan, which was implemented the following year, called for the relocation of about 10 percent of headquarters personnel to field offices around the country. Ashcroft told Justice Department staff, "The war on terrorism will not be fought in Washington but in the field by agents." While the Justice Department itself concentrated on updating its own technology, the FBI would make counterterrorism its first priority.

The shakeup was followed in 2002 by the FBI's first new investigative guidelines in twenty-five years. Its agents gained power to monitor people at any public event or place, if they suspected a terrorist plot. Supporters of the changes argued that the FBI could not fight terrorism with practices designed to combat regular crime. Opponents said that the new powers gave the FBI the ability to spy on Americans and ignore their civil liberties.

At his trial, Reid pleaded guilty to trying to blow up the plane. He said that he was a soldier for Osama bin Laden and an enemy of the United States. Judge William Young told him, "You are not a soldier—you are a terrorist." In January 2003, Reid was sentenced to life in prison.

Uncovering Threads

Also in 2003, a group many believe to have been an al-Qaeda "sleeper cell" was discovered in Buffalo, New York. Six American citizens whose families had arrived from Yemen in the 1960s and 1970s were charged with "providing material support to the al-Qaeda terrorist organization." They had visited an al-Qaeda training camp

in Afghanistan in 2001, before the September 11 attacks. The government argued that they planned a future attack on the United States, although nothing linked them to a specific threat. They were all sent to jail for between seven and ten years.

In 2005, authorities broke up a Bronx, New York-based scheme to provide support to al-Qaeda for training terrorists. They also deported a sixteen-year-old Bangladeshi girl who had lived in Queens, New York, since age five. The FBI learned that Tashnuba Hayder visited an Internet chat room hosted by an Islamic cleric who encouraged suicide bombers. They thought there was a threat that the girl might become a suicide bomber. After

▼ A Baghdad statue of Saddam Hussein is toppled in 2003, marking the end of his brutal and long regime.

being detained for seven weeks, she was released on the condition that she return to Bangladesh immediately.

Islamists have attacked many countries in addition to the United States, and the struggle against their terrorism is an international effort. After the 9/11 attacks, not only did a wide range of countries join Operation Enduring Freedom, many also arrested people in their own countries who had links to al-Qaeda. In Germany, associates of the 9/11 hijackers who had lived in that country were arrested.

Attack on Iraq

In January 2003, the United States expanded the war on terror when President Bush identified Iraq as a part of an "axis of evil." Vice president Dick Cheney claimed that Iraqi president Saddam Hussein had given refuge to al-Qaeda. Secretary of State Colin Powell made the same claim when he addressed the United Nations Security Council about the need for military action against Iraq. He said that the al-Qaeda operative Abu Musab al-Zarqawi had been allowed to create a terrorist training camp in Iraq. He went on, "Al-Qaeda affiliates, based in Baghdad, now coordinate the movement of people, money, and supplies into and throughout Iraq. . . and they've now

been operating freely in the capital for more than eight months." The assertion was challenged at the time by many critics, and the government itself later became less certain of a link between Iraq and al-Qaeda.

The administration also said that Hussein had weapons of mass destruction (WMD). The United Nations had sent investigators to Iraq to look for such weapons in 2002, but they did not find anything.

In March 2003, the United States, in alliance with Britain and many other countries—but few other major world powers—invaded Iraq. The invasion toppled Hussein, but unlike the attack on the Taliban it lacked wide international support. France and Germany, for example, opposed it. Meanwhile, millions of demonstrators around the world protested what they saw as an illegal invasion.

The invasion of Iraq and the subsequent U.S.-led occupation enraged many Islamists

The U.S.-led coalition kept a large military force in Iraq to facilitate the country's transition to self rule. In January 2005, Iraq held its first general election since 1958, and in October of that year, it held a referendum on a new constitution for the country.

Insurgency in Iraq

The invasion of Iraq and the subsequent U.S.-led occupation enraged many Islamists. After Saddam was toppled from power, extremist groups—including Islamists from states such as Syria, and Iraqis loyal to Saddam Hussein—launched an insurgency. They attacked the occupying troops and local police forces, assassinated members of the interim government, and made terror attacks on Iraqis with views they oppose. They also kidnapped and murdered hostages, not only from Western countries but also from Muslim nations such as Algeria.

Some intelligence experts believe that one of their leaders, the Jordanian-born Abu Musab al-Zarqawi, is an al-Qaeda operative. Others argue that he operates virtually independently. The United States has offered a reward of $25 million for his capture.

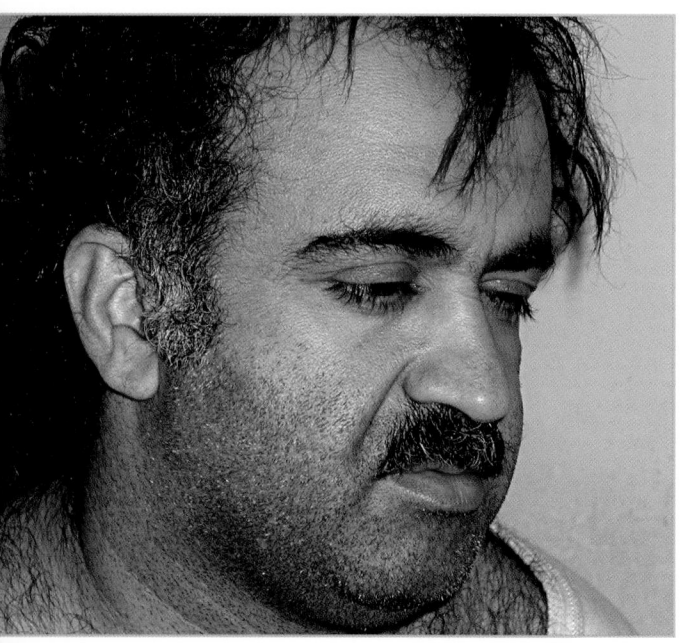

▼ Khalid Sheikh Mohammed, pictured after his arrest in March 2003, was the al-Qaeda mastermind behind the 9/11 attacks.

In addition to opposing Western occupation of an Islamic state, some insurgents also had another motive. Under Saddam, Sunni Muslims governed Iraq. With the dictator gone, the Shiite Muslims who make up the majority in the south and the west of the country would have far more economic and political power. In September 2005, al-Zarqawi announced the beginning of a new campaign of terrorist attacks against all Iraqi Shiites. Some observers believed that the insurgents sought to defeat Shiite political influence.

Attacks Overseas

Some experts believe that the war in Iraq may have inspired more terrorist attacks outside the country. Two of the United States' chief allies in Iraq, Spain and Great Britain, have been the target of terrorists. In March 2004, bombs blew up rush-hour commuter trains in Madrid, Spain's capital, killing more than two hundred people. Al-Qaeda released a statement saying that the attack was a response to the war in Iraq. When Spanish police raided an apartment where suspected terrorists were living, the suspects blew themselves up rather than be arrested.

The Islamist suicide bombings in London in July 2005, meanwhile, alarmed European security services, which after the Madrid bombings had set up a center in Brussels, Belgium, to share information about terrorism. The four bombers had no connection with any known terrorist cells, making them virtually impossible to identify or prevent. Ayman al-Zawahiri appeared in a video praising the attacks, but many experts believed that the tape did not prove a direct link between the bombers and al-Qaeda.

Difficult Questions

Like the United States, Europe faces difficult questions about combating Islamist terrorism. In the Netherlands, for example, which is known for its tolerance, tough new laws were passed to allow police to detain suspects without charge. They were a reaction to the murder of filmmaker Theo Van Gogh in November 2004. Van Gogh was killed by a member of the Islamist Hofstad group after he made a movie critical of radical Islam. After the July 2005 bombings in Britain, a long tradition of free speech was overturned by new laws making it possible to deport Islamist preachers who advocate violence.

While some people remain troubled by the moral dilemmas raised by the war on terror, the fight against Islamist terrorism has had concrete successes, including the arrests of major al-Qaeda leaders such as Khalid Sheikh Mohammed. Al-Qaeda and other radical Islamic terrorist groups, however, remain highly dangerous. The United States and its allies seek to combat the danger while preserving the very freedoms that Islamist terrorists set out to destroy.

The Changing Shape of al-Qaeda

Counterterrorism experts warn that one of the problems with combating Islamist terrorism is the way al-Qaeda has changed since the U.S-led attacks on its Afghan bases in 2001. Some observers believe that it has developed a structure that makes it very different from traditional terrorist groups. Its loose structure makes it far harder to monitor or infiltrate—or prevent from launching its attacks.

Rather than being an organization with a large membership, al-Qaeda may now be restricted largely to Osama bin Laden and other leaders, such as Ayman al-Zawahiri. They may coordinate a network for funding and advising small terrorist groups around the world. Instead of centrally planning attacks, as they did for 9/11, they leave operational details to the local cells. Al-Qaeda may or may not finance such operations.

An example of the new approach may have come with the London bombings of July 2005. Al-Jazeera later aired a videotape of one of the bombers, Mohammad Sidique Khan, trying to justify the attacks. The same tape also included film of Ayman al-Zawahiri celebrating the London blasts. Experts were dubious, however, that the tape proved that al-Qaeda was directly linked to the attacks.

Time Line

1979	January: A revolution brings an Islamist government to power in Iran.
1991	Osama bin Laden moves to Sudan.
1993	February 26: Islamists bomb the World Trade Center, New York City.
1996	Osama bin Laden moves to Taliban-controlled Afghanistan.
1998	Bin Laden calls for Muslims to attack all Americans. August: Al-Qaeda attacks U.S. embassies in Tanzania and Kenya.
2000	October: Al-Qaeda suicide bombers attack the USS *Cole* in Yemen.
2001	September 11: Al-Qaeda terrorists crash two hijacked airliners into the World Trade Center, New York City, and a third into the Pentagon, in Washington, D.C. A fourth aircraft crashes in Pennsylvania. October 7: U.S. and international forces attack Afghanistan in Operation Enduring Freedom. October: The U.S. Patriot Act becomes law. December: An Islamist bomber fails to detonate a shoe bomb on an airplane above the Atlantic Ocean.
2002	October: Islamist terrorists blow up a nightclub in Bali, Indonesia.
2003	March: The United States and its allies invade Iraq. Key al-Qaeda leaders are arrested in Pakistan.
2004	March 11: Islamists blow up four commuter trains in Madrid, Spain.
2005	July 7: Islamist suicide bombers blow up three subway trains and a bus in London, England. September: Insurgents in Iraq declare a new terrorist campaign. October 1: Islamists bomb three restaurants in Bali, Indonesia.

Glossary

capitalism: an economic system based on private property and the making of profits.

cleric: a member of the clergy, such as a priest or imam.

communism: an economic system based on collective ownership and regulation by the state.

extremist: someone who holds radical beliefs and rejects any form of compromise.

fundamentalist: a person who believes in strictly following the basic principles of a religion or other set of beliefs.

hijacker: someone who takes over an airplane, ship, or other form of transportation and forces it to go to a destination he or she chooses.

insurgent: a person who takes place in an unlawful uprising against civic authority.

Islamist: a Muslim who believes that Islam should be the basis of all forms of government and culture.

jihad: in Islam, a battle waged as a religious duty; used both for a personal battle against religious doubt and for battles against peceived enemies of Islam.

Koran: the holy book of Islam.

monotheism: the belief that there is only one god; Christianity, Islam, and Judaism are all monotheistic religions.

mosque: a building used by Muslims for worship.

mujahideen: Islamic guerrilla fighters, particularly in the Middle East and Afghanistan.

nationalist: a person who believes in the importance of his or her nation and its culture and interests.

partition: the legal division of a country into two or more nations.

radical: having extreme views; also, a person who holds such views.

secular: nonreligious; involved with concerns of the natural world as opposed to the afterlife or the supernatural.

sharia: a system of laws based on the Koran and other Islamic teachings.

Further Reading

Books

Block, Evelyn B. *September 11, 2001: A Day in History*. XLibris Corporation, 2003.

Gunderson, Cory. *Islamic Fundamentalism* (World in Conflict. Middle East). Abdo and Daughters Publishing, 2003.

Harris, Nathaniel. *Terrorism* (21st Century Issues). World Almanac Library, 2004.

Mintzer, Richard. *Keeping the Peace: The U.S. Military Responds to Terror* (Spirit of America, a Nation Responds to the Events of September 11, 2001). Chelsea House Publications, 2002.

Shostak, Arthur B. *Turning Point: The Rocky Road To Peace And Reconstruction: Beyond 9/11 and the Iraq War* (Defeating Terrorism, Developing Dreams). Chelsea House Publications, 2004.

Stewart, Gail B. *America Under Attack: September 11, 2001* (Terrorism Library Series). Lucent Books, 2002.

Valdez, Angela. *We the People: The U.S. Government's United Response Against Terror* (Spirit of America, a Nation Responds to the Events of September 11, 2001).Chelsea House Publications, 2002.

Wheeler, Jill C. *September 11, 2001: The Day That Changed America* (War on Terrorism). Abdo and Daughters Publishing, 2002.

Young, Mitchell (ed.) *The War on Terrorism* (Turning Points in World History). Greenhaven Press, 2003.

Web Sites

The National Commission on Terrorist Attacks Upon the United States
www.9-11commission.gov/

September11news.com
www.september11news.com/

The New York Times: The 9/11 Records
www.nytimes.com/pages/nyregion/nyregionspecial3/

BBC News In Depth: Investigating al-Qaeda
news.bbc.co.uk/1/hi/in_depth/world/2001/war_on_terror/

CNN.com: War Against Terror
edition.cnn.com/SPECIALS/2001/trade.center/

Index

Page numbers in *italics* indicate photographs or diagrams.